To Claudia, a beautiful light,
Wishing you
ever so much
Faith,
Hope,
&
Love,
Kay

# Endorsements

A book you will never forget! Just thinking of Kay's life and how she has served others regardless of her own pain brings tears of reverence for such an indomitable, highly talented woman! Read MY WALK OF FAITH, HOPE, AND LOVE. Allow it to inspire you to achieve greater heights! Your life will never be the same because Kay demonstrates the effectiveness of living in attunement with "I can do all things through Christ who strengthens me." Philippians 4-13

**Nancy B. Detweiler, Author**


After reading **My Walk of Faith, Hope, and Love,** I am inspired and uplifted. This is a beautifully touching memoir from a gifted spiritual woman. The journey Kay takes us on is honest and touching -- one we can all benefit from. Finding one's truth, listening to *inner* messages we often are too busy or fearful to hear -- and understanding the connection of music to healing, are messages Kay shares.

Kay guides the reader in music's therapy, using her own painful and emotional battle with cancer. So many people would benefit from reading about and embracing this modality... I have worked with Kay since 2006 to address her current severe spinal conditions, performing Pilates based rehabilitation. I have seen firsthand- -- her strength and spirit -- and benefited from both. I feel this book will allow her valuable story and insight to help many others.

**Julie Williamson, MS PT, Pilates Rehabilitation Specialist.**

This wonderful memoir, written with such honest emotion and crystal recollection, shares the experiences of a young woman with breast cancer who faces seemingly unsurmountable obstacles with courage, insight, and understanding. The reader will share a vast range of feelings as Kay Johnson, at age 31, faces the reality of breast cancer, the impact of the surgical amputation, the fear, doubts, and vulnerabilities that are ultimately addressed by her faith in God, her love of music, her appreciation of her family's love – and John Denver. Her incredible growth, from an obedient, compliant, accepting young woman to an inspired, informed, assertive young woman is an experience worth sharing with anyone who faces difficult decisions, questions feelings and fears, and seeks meaningful answers – in other words, all of us. This is a memoir of courage and resolution that will bring inspiration and solace to the reader who values Faith, Hope, and Love.

**Claudia Z. Le, MBA**
**Comprehensive Breast Center Consultations**

# My Walk of Faith, Hope, and Love

Dr. Kay Johnson-Gentile

Copyright © 2016 Dr. Kay Johnson-Gentile.

All rights reserved. No part of this book may be used or reproduced by any means, graphic, electronic, or mechanical, including photocopying, recording, taping or by any information storage retrieval system without the written permission of the author except in the case of brief quotations embodied in critical articles and reviews.

Balboa Press books may be ordered through booksellers or by contacting:

Balboa Press
A Division of Hay House
1663 Liberty Drive
Bloomington, IN 47403
www.balboapress.com
1 (877) 407-4847

Because of the dynamic nature of the Internet, any web addresses or links contained in this book may have changed since publication and may no longer be valid. The views expressed in this work are solely those of the author and do not necessarily reflect the views of the publisher, and the publisher hereby disclaims any responsibility for them.

The author of this book does not dispense medical advice or prescribe the use of any technique as a form of treatment for physical, emotional, or medical problems without the advice of a physician, either directly or indirectly. The intent of the author is only to offer information of a general nature to help you in your quest for emotional and spiritual well-being. In the event you use any of the information in this book for yourself, which is your constitutional right, the author and the publisher assume no responsibility for your actions.

Any people depicted in stock imagery provided by Thinkstock are models, and such images are being used for illustrative purposes only.
Certain stock imagery © Thinkstock.

Print information available on the last page.

ISBN: 978-1-5043-5688-6 (sc)
ISBN: 978-1-5043-5690-9 (hc)
ISBN: 978-1-5043-5689-3 (e)

Library of Congress Control Number: 2016907744

Balboa Press rev. date: 05/21/2016

This book is dedicated with love to
my family – especially Bill, Chris, Tim, Mom, and Dad.

## Acknowledgements

This "story of the heart" takes place during a three-year period (1975 through April 1978). It is about my challenging bout with breast cancer and how music – especially the music of John Denver – helped me overcome depression and aid my healing. John and I became friends, talking on the phone and then meeting in person after one of his Buffalo concerts.

I would sign on to become a volunteer for the New York State Division of the American Cancer Society (ACS), eventually being asked to direct a Volunteer Music Therapy Pilot Project for Kids with Cancer at Roswell Park Cancer Institute in Buffalo, New York. For my work for the ACS, I was selected as *One of Ten Outstanding Young Women of America in 1977.*

My *can-do story* will hopefully help people see the connection between emotions and music, as well as the therapeutic properties of this amazing medium. Learning to utilize, effectively, this powerful tool – music -- could make the world a kinder, more compassionate place to live. As you read my book, you will see what I mean.

This project could not have been completed without the help of some very special and important people.

First and foremost, thanks are extended to my husband, Ron Gilmore, for giving me ideas on how to make my text more real, succinct, and readable. He was my primary editor as well as the person who made photographs, taken nearly fifty years ago, come to life once again.

Because of my spinal disability and pain issues, Ron also provided continual care during some very dark hours. Because of his loving ministrations, I was able to complete my book.

Second, thanks to my son, Christopher Alan Johnson, for encouraging me to become the strong woman I was meant to be. He was also extremely helpful with this book, providing constructive criticism and suggestions that were insightful and useful.

I want to also thank my writing mentor, Carolyn Walker. I first met Carolyn when I signed up with Writer's Digest to have a critique done of the first chapter of this book. Carolyn was assigned to work with me, and she opened my eyes to so many things about writing, including my talent for memoir.

Thanks to my family and friends, especially my sister, Lois Kaznica, and brother, Rex Burgher, for reading and rereading my stories about this period of time in my life. They helped me with memory issues as well as offered constructive criticism.

Thanks to my lifelong friend Cheryl Ludwig for her photographic talents. There is no doubt in my mind that Cheryl's photos made this book come alive.

Of course, I want to thank John Denver, whose beautiful spirit is alive and well and still uplifting and inspiring me, as well as new generations of listeners. Thank you, John, for continuing to bring us all so much joy.

Finally, thanks to everyone at Balboa Press who put all of the parts together to create my precious book, **My Walk of Faith, Hope, and Love.** Words are incapable of expressing my gratitude.

Be blessed, dear readers.

Kay

*Writing my story My Walk of Faith, Hope, and Love*

## Contents

1. The Setting of my Story ............................................................ 1
2. My Life is Changed Forever ..................................................... 6
3. I Was Not Consulted About This ........................................... 12
4. The Love of a Father ............................................................... 15
5. Face to Face With My Truth .................................................. 18
6. Home, At Last! ........................................................................ 23
7. The Transforming Miracle of Music ..................................... 30
8. Understanding the Healing Properties of Dreams ............ 37
9. John Denver and I Connect ................................................... 41
10. My Early Years And Music ................................................... 46
11. How the Ancients Viewed Music ......................................... 52
12. Volunteering for The American Cancer Society (ACS) .... 55
13. Beginning My Walk of Faith, Hope, and Love .................. 71
14. Epilogue ................................................................................... 77

*Me with my trusty guitar*

# Chapter One
## The Setting of my Story

*Musical training is a more potent instrument than
any other because rhythm and harmony find
their way into the inward places of the soul.*
Plato, *The Republic*

Nineteen seventy-five is a year I will always remember. It was the year the revolutionary movie, *One Flew Over the Cuckoo's Nest*, took *all* the big prizes including Best Picture at the Academy Awards. It was the year *Saturday Night Live* premiered on NBC television. In sports, the amazing Billie Jean King and Arthur Ashe were Wimbledon champions. And *The Way We Were*, recorded by Barbra Streisand, was the song of the year.

Gerald Ford was president of the United States with former Governor of New York, Nelson Rockefeller, serving as second in command. Our President escaped two assassination attempts, and on April 24 the Vietnamese War officially ended. *All in the Family* and *Laverne and Shirley* were top TV shows, and Freddie Fender was taking the world by storm with his big hit, *Before the Next Teardrop Falls*.

It was also the year I discovered I had breast cancer – something I *never* believed would happen -- not to me. But it did happen, and the experience would change my life forever.

In many ways, my cancer story is similar to thousands of others, but there are at least three important differences. First was the major role *music* played in my recovery, especially the music of 1970s Superstar, John Denver. Denver's music not only brought me out of severe depression but helped me heal from the physical and mental ravages of a potentially fatal disease.

The second difference was my becoming Coordinator of a Volunteer Music Therapy Pilot Project for Children and Adolescents with Cancer. This cutting edge project was sponsored by the New York State Division of the American Cancer Society (ACS). Dr. James Wallace, then Director of Cancer Control at Roswell Park Cancer Institute, was the brains behind the project.

The third was the effect cancer had on me as a woman. Before this experience, I was not very assertive or bold. I felt quite content going along with my husband's desires and decisions. I was dependent on him, thinking that was appropriate behavior for a good wife. As naïve as it sounds, in my twenties, it is what I believed.

That was also true regarding my spiritual and religious beliefs. I had not thought through important religious doctrine and developed beliefs of my own. I did not have my own voice. I did not speak my own truth. I had not yet created an authentic identity.

As I look back on this time, I know my soul was doing its best to push me in a more independent and assertive direction. But I was not listening to this *inner voice,* so concerned about my womanhood. The only indication I had that something was not right was a growing anxiety and feeling of discontent. It was an inner knowing that there just had to be more to life than I was experiencing.

My story begins in early November 1974. My husband, Bill Johnson, and I were living with our two small boys in Lockport, New York, a small town in Niagara County situated on the historic Erie Canal about 23 miles from Niagara Falls.

It was shortly before midnight, and after a long day, I was following my nightly pattern of reading before drifting off to sleep. Out of nowhere, this thought impressed itself on my mind -- you need to do a breast self-examination now. This intuitive message was accompanied with an overwhelming feeling of urgency -- a sort of now or never feeling. It was scary.

I had learned to follow through on these intuitive messages since personal experience had proved them worthy of both attention and action. In fact, I had come to believe I had a guardian angel out there communicating with me, keeping me on a path of health and happiness.

These premonitions began happening a few years after Bill and I were married. It was the middle of August 1965. I was a young, perky 22-year-old who loved yearly excursions to the Erie County Fair.

Bill had purchased raffle tickets hoping we might win one of the twenty prizes being given away. In the best of all worlds, we would win one of the two Motorola 21-inch console TV sets. Our current TV was quite old and desperately in need of replacement. In order to win it was necessary to be present at the evening drawing. Unfortunately, the drawing did not take place until 9:00 PM.

Since we were planning to be at the fair all day, we did not believe staying that late would be a problem. However, after visiting nearly every specialized exhibit and agricultural display and riding many of the carnival rides, we were feeling so exhausted and tired we decided to head home. Our leaving early meant we would not have a chance at the prizes.

On the way out of the fairgrounds, I had my *first* intuitive message. I found myself in a rather dreamy, other-worldly state of mind with a strong impression I was about to win something. "You need to stay at the fair as you are going to win a big prize in the raffle," a voice whispered to me.

This was the *first* time I had ever heard this inner voice, I looked around wondering if someone at the fair had spoken to me. I realized this was not the case. This voice was *within me*. I was not in the least bit frightened. "Wow," I said to myself, softly, "this is something new."

After a quick discussion with Bill, we decided to stay. It was a good thing we did because we won one of the Motorola TVs. We were both delighted, and I became a believer in my intuitive flashes.

Now my intuition was telling me a breast self-exam was necessary. I knew it was important to do it.

When I touched my left breast, I discovered a rather large lump. A surge of fear ran through my body. I was shocked. I remember thinking that the lump must have been in my breast quite a while because of its size. How could I have missed it, I thought to myself? I did these exams fairly regularly. How?

I knew I needed to see my doctor, so the following day I made an appointment. Dr. Tokarz said the lump appeared to be benign. However, to be on the safe side he gave me the name of a prominent Buffalo female breast surgeon, Nancy Stubbe, explaining it would be best for me to get her expert opinion.

Beginning to feel more anxious and nervous about this whole incident, I called Dr. Stubbe's office later the same day. Her secretary was very helpful. I was grateful I could see the doctor within the week.

Stubbe's office was in Buffalo about 35 miles from my home. I had a friend come with me. Our plan was to take advantage of our time in Buffalo with a lunch out after my appointment. My friend also provided moral support since the feelings of urgency and nervousness I had experienced when discovering the lump seemed to continue hanging around. I just could not throw these impressions of gloom no matter what I did.

After a thorough examination from the surgeon, I was told I had found a fibroid tumor. Dr. Stubbe said not to worry since tumors like this were *always* benign. However, since the appearance of fibroids in the breast can increase the chances of breast cancer, she felt we should be prudent and have surgery to remove it. Arrangements were made to have the surgery performed in late January 1975, shortly before my thirty-second birthday.

My parents, then living in the Midwest, decided to come up to help my husband and me with our two active preschool boys, Timothy who was four and Christopher who was nearly three. I was happy and relieved they were coming.

## Chapter Two
## My Life is Changed Forever

*After silence, that which comes nearest to
expressing the inexpressible is music.*
Aldous Huxley

With everything in place, I was admitted to the Buffalo General Hospital the evening before my surgery. I was told my operation would begin promptly at 8:30 AM and take 30 to 40 minutes. I would be back in my room before lunch and able to go home in the early afternoon.

I was assured this was a routine procedure. **The possibility of having cancer was *never* discussed.** Before drifting off to sleep, I said a brief prayer asking God to guide the surgeon's hands and bring me safely through tomorrow's events.

I always felt better after praying. Raised Southern Baptist, my family always thought of Sunday as God's day. Attending Sunday school and church were what you did on Sunday. Most people in my hometown of Moberly, Missouri, were church goers. It was just the way it was back then.

Local stores were closed on Sundays. And though movie theaters were open, there were not many other non-church activities taking place.

My family also attended Wednesday night prayer services. Dad taught the adult Sunday school class and was a church deacon. Mom was president of the women's association. I became our church organist at the age of 12. In addition,

My Walk of Faith, Hope, and Love

I directed two children's choirs, and in the summer taught vacation Bible school.

My sister and brother, though younger than me, were active in both Sunday school and Bible school. All of my family could recite the 66 books of the Protestant Bible and knew numerous verses by heart. We were an active church family.

When Bill and I married, I decided to switch churches. Bill and his family were Presbyterians. We decided to be married in his church, the University Presbyterian Church, right across the street from the University at Buffalo campus.

When we moved to Lockport, New York, in 1974, we simply changed churches becoming members of the First Presbyterian Church there. Lockport Pres, as the locals called it, was a wonderful church and attracted many young married couples like ourselves. This was in part due to the excellent activities at the church. There was always something going on that was family-oriented. Bill and I liked that.

We became active at Lockport Pres. I sang in the chancel choir, directed the cherub choir, and was the assistant organist. Bill taught Sunday school and was a member of the church's governing body.

After having a near-death experience when I was twenty-five I began believing in the concept of reincarnation. I had an ectopic pregnancy emergency while teaching my 6th-grade class at St. Leo's Elementary School. My fallopian tube ruptured because my baby was growing there and simply grew too large for the small enclosure. I began hemorrhaging internally though none of us realized this initially.

Bu the time I arrived at the Women and Children's Hospital in Buffalo I was nearly dead. Of course, I lost the baby and nearly lost my life. But the surgical expertise of Maurice Dewey saved me. From that time forward I was referred to by him as *The Miracle Lady*.

During this shocking experience, I found myself out of my body -- looking down on myself writhing in pain. Now they call this an *out of body experience,* but when it happened to me in the late 1960s, it was simply something that was NOT discussed. Yet I absolutely knew all would be well. No matter what happened – even death – it would be okay. This experience convinced me that life continues after death.

My sister-in-law, Janet Long, introduced me to the work of metaphysical healer Edgar Cayce, an advocate of reincarnation and karma. After studying more about these interesting concepts, I realized they provided answers I was looking for.

Reincarnation tells us that our current lives contain the seeds of our former selves. Everything we are today is because of lessons learned and deeds done in prior lives. So a musical prodigy like Mozart had studied music and musical composing in the past. When he was born in his latest life as Mozart, he brought with him talents and accomplishments from prior lives. In reality, he had already developed or earned these talents. We saw him as a child prodigy because we had no knowledge of his past lives.

I had always been troubled by people or children who died young. It did not seem fair that their one chance at life would get cut off by an early death. Reincarnation took away my feelings of unfairness since I realized these people would have other lives. Their current life was not their only chance at living.

Maybe they died early because spiritual understanding was attained early on, and they had nothing else they needed to do or learn. Or possibly a family member they were deeply connected to needed to experience a loss in order for them to grow spiritually. The bottom line is these people will live again. They will live to serve again.

In addition to my interest and study of reincarnation, I began exploring other religions and religious concepts. Though I remained Christian, I felt strongly there was more I needed to know. Study and research proved helpful. I was finding answers that resonated strongly with me. I would eventually become a follower of Christian mystic philosophy and practices. But that would come much later during my senior years and my work at the St. Joseph Center for Spirituality.

Yes, my belief in God was important to me. Praying was a way to talk to Him. It was a way for us to get to know each other better. So the night before my surgery, I definitely needed to have a little conversation with my Heavenly Father.

After praying I drifted off to sleep. I awakened shortly before my surgery prep the following morning. I recall being rolled into the operating room. When the gurney came to a halt, I looked up at the wall clock. It was exactly 8:30 AM. My anesthesia was ready to be administered. "Well," I quietly said to myself, "they certainly keep to their schedules for surgery."

That was the last thing I remember before the anesthesia took effect. I was now completely unconscious to the traumatic events that were about to unfold.

I next remember waking up in recovery and realizing it was *dark outside*. I was very confused. Though still groggy, I surmised that darkness plus the time on the wall clock meant it must be 8 PM. But how could that be? The clock must be wrong. My surgery was supposed to take less than an hour. I was supposed to be back in Lockport now. Why was it dark? What in the world was going on?

I called out for help. A nurse walked over to my bed and peered down at me with a look that bordered on dread. I felt she did not want to talk with me. "But why, " I thought.

She immediately said she could not discuss my case – only the doctor could do that. She added that he would be with me soon.

I asked her, "Do you know that your wall clock is not working correctly?"

Looking at me straight on, she said, "Why do you think that?"

I quickly responded, "I just don't get it. My surgery was only supposed to take thirty to forty-five minutes. I was told I would be home by now. It's late. It's dark. What is going on?"

My talking became quite fast. It was obvious I was upset, but most of all I was confused – really bewildered.

She said, "Well, first of all, it is eight o'clock at night. Your surgery indeed lasted longer than was initially anticipated. The doctor on duty has been called and will be here within five minutes. He can explain everything. I simply am not allowed to do that."

She left, hurriedly. I was more confused than ever!

Within a short time, a doctor was by my side explaining that a very unfortunate event had occurred during what had become a nearly nine-hour surgical procedure. After removing the benign tumor, the doctors discovered a malignant one beneath it.

My surgeon had talked with my husband and parents by phone from the operating room, explaining the unexpected situation. She gave them possible options of what could happen next.

The decision needing to be dealt with immediately was whether to perform radical or less radical surgery. Stubbe felt the radical approach (Halsted Radical Mastectomy) would provide me with the best chance of surviving long-term.

However, that procedure would be the most disfiguring, as not only would the breast be removed but the pectoral muscles in the chest and numerous nodes as well.

My surgeon felt it necessary. She believed that since I was already under anesthesia, it was in my best interest to perform the Radical Mastectomy immediately. Letting me make the decision was not a good idea since time was of the essence. My family agreed with her thinking.

Dr. Stubbe began removing my left breast and then extracted the pectoral muscles on the left side of my chest along with a number of lymph nodes she felt were problematic.

Because of the large amount of muscle and nodes removed, I was told my left arm might swell up permanently, a condition called lymphedema. If that happened – and it often did in cases like mine -- the use of my left arm would be severely limited.

If I was fortunate enough to not be afflicted with lymphedema, it would still take intense, consistent physical therapy to counteract the effects of the radical surgery and get my left arm back to a useable condition. Hearing this news was devastating!

I was a musician who played piano, guitar, and organ. I remember thinking, "What does she mean I could not use my left arm effectively again?"

Suddenly I could not get my breath. I gasped over and over. I felt light headed like I could pass out.

I remember thinking, passing out would be good. I would not be able to think or reason. That would be wonderful. Right now I wanted *oblivion*.

Suddenly everything went black. But only for a few minutes.

"How very unfortunate," I thought when I come to. "I want to be unconscious for a long time – a very long time!"

## Chapter Three
### I Was Not Consulted About This

*Music is what tells us that the human race is greater than we realize."*
Napoleon Bonaparte

To make matters worse, the doctors had cut so deeply into the left side of my chest (removing everything down to the ribcage) there was no skin left to cover the wound. To remedy this, they performed a skin graft, taking a patch of skin from my right thigh to cover the surgical wound. It would take months for my graft to heal.

And if all this was not enough, within the week I was to begin nine months of rigorous chemotherapy treatments. Unfortunately, utilizing these aggressive measures still provided no guarantees I would survive cancer.

**Never** had I been hit with such shocking news – a real Armageddon experience. My entire life had changed in a few short hours – and I had not been part of the decision making! I had not had the opportunity to think through my options and chose what was best for me.

Realizing this blatant oversight by the medical profession was unbearable to me for months – even years. However, in the 1970s, this was the way breast surgery was conducted. I always hated the word victim – but this procedure WAS indeed victimizing!

I soon found myself in a state of denial. I really believed that someone would tell me this horror movie I was living was a dream, nothing else.

Shortly before 11 PM, I was able to leave recovery. As I was wheeled onto the third floor and into the room that was to be my home for the next few weeks, I was relieved to see the other bed was empty. I could not imagine a conversation with a roommate. The nurses took a few minutes getting me settled. They wanted to be sure I knew what button to press if I needed help. I only wished there was a *God button*.

Bill and my parents walked into the room. Their faces were swollen and red. It was obvious all three had been crying.

"What a long, traumatic day for us all," I said, holding back what seemed to be a barrage of tears.

No one knew what to say to me. Bill looked exhausted but walked over and stood right beside the bed. He bent over and kissed me on the check. His voice was shaky, "We are all so happy you made it through. Dr. Stubbe believes everything looks good, and we, ah …"

Dad interrupted, "You are going to be fine, my little princess, just fine. And Mom and I will be with you as long as you need us. We are prepared to stay two months or more – whatever you need."

I simply said, "Thank you. I love you all and am so glad you are here. You must be exhausted, though."

Everyone in the room avoided the C word -- cancer. Mom and Dad did not use this word for the next two years. They referred to my breast cancer as my *sickness* or my *condition*.

The nurse came into the room again. "We need to close down shop for the night," she said. "But you can visit Kay again beginning at 11 in the morning."

It was obvious Dad did not want to leave me. In fact, he told me he would be happy to stay with me and sleep in the chair in the room. I insisted he go home and get some good rest.

When everyone was gone and I was left alone in my room, I let the barrage of tears come forth. In fact, there was no way this tidal wave of sorrow could have been prevented.

However, I still kept telling myself this was a bad joke. Tomorrow Dr. Stubbe would tell me they just wanted to see how I would handle this horrid scenario. I knew she would do this – tomorrow. I just had to get through this night.

## Chapter Four
### The Love of a Father

*Life is like a beautiful melody, only
the lyrics are messed up.*
Hans Christian Andersen

Dad was back at the hospital the next morning at 9:30 AM. Though visiting hours did not begin until 11 AM, my day nurse, Barbara, let him into my room early. My dad became a very popular visitor as the days wore on. All of my nurses came to love him. This was because of his real concern for me, and the way he sacrificed his own needs for mine.

On this particular day, Dad asked me if I would like him to be present when my doctor made her rounds. I immediately responded, yes. I was having so much trouble remembering everything the doctor told me. Having dad there would be such help.

By 1 PM the doctor still had not come. I was not able to eat yet, as it was too soon after my surgery, but I was concerned about Dad. He had not eaten anything since his breakfast in Lockport hours before. I suggested he go for lunch in the hospital cafeteria. He refused though he looked both tired and hungry.

He was afraid if he left he would miss my doctor's visit. Instead, he purchased candy bars from one of the vending machines on our floor. Lunch for dad consisted of a Baby Ruth and a Three Musketeers candy bar.. But he was right by my side when my doctor arrived at 2:30. I was **so** happy he was there.

The nurses touched by his caring, nurturing manner would say to me, "You are so lucky to have a dad who loves you so much. My goodness, he would do anything for you. Just anything!"

This was actually the beginning of my seeing Dad in a brand new more loving way. We had been at odds since my marriage to Bill. Dad had not wanted me to marry Bill because Bill was a juvenile diabetic. He was afraid Bill would die—leaving me with two small boys and needing to fend for myself.

During the days immediately following my surgery, it was Dad who was my daytime visitor. He was the person I talked to about my "new life." Sometimes we were simply quiet, but he was always there.

He would often stay five or six hours, sometimes longer. Mom was, of course, home with our boys. Bill visited me when his workday ended, but his visits were short ones. From a logical perspective, I could completely understand this. I realized Bill must be exhausted by this whole ordeal. And after working hard all day, it had to be very difficult for him to then spend time in a hospital. Bill also knew that Dad was with me. But emotions are not ruled by logic. And I was feeling emotional, not logical. I just felt hurt by Bill's short visits.

A few days after my surgery, my day nurse, Barbara, was in my room early at 5:30 AM. She smiled at me and said, "Today we need to get you up on your feet and walking. It will not feel that great. But we need to do it. I also think it would be a good idea to get you up now, giving you some practice before your dad comes. I know he will be so happy to see you moving. What do you think?"

"Yes," I said to her, "that's a great idea. Let's do it."

She called for an additional nurse, and the two of them got me sitting up on the bed with my legs dangling over the edge. I stayed there a few minutes. "Now Kay, you must look straight ahead," said the head nurse. "Do not look down, or you will feel nauseous and dizzy. Got it? You are to look straight ahead."

"Got it," I said.

The nurses got on both sides of me and lifted me up. I felt so light headed I had to sit down again. I was shocked at how weak I felt. We tried again. This time, it worked. I walked slowly, looking straight ahead. I did feel nauseous but continued walking anyway. The nausea subsided as I kept my eyes straight ahead. When I returned to my room, I was exhausted.

When Dad arrived about two hours later, both nurses came in again. "We have something to show you, Mr. Burgher. A little surprise," they said beaming.

They got on both sides of me, and once again away we went. I felt minimal nausea. I was also much less exhausted when our walk ended. My dad was thrilled. I was, too.

## Chapter Five
### Face to Face With My Truth

*Without music, life would be a blank to me.*
Jane Austen, *Emma*

The fourth day after surgery, Dr. Stubbe needed to change my surgical bandages. This was my moment of truth. I was very nervous. The doctor said before she began that this would be emotionally painful. Hoping to make the situation a bit less hurtful she added, "Kay you need to remember that although the incision area will look pretty bad right now, as time passes it will look better and better."

I wanted to snap my fingers and like magic be somewhere else. Somewhere beautiful. Somewhere without pain. But I was stuck here forced to see "my truth," even though I didn't want to.

When the bandages were off and I garnered the courage to look at the incision, my throat constricted. My heart started pounding so loudly I thought everyone in the room could hear it. I wanted to scream, "My God, my body has been desecrated. Half of it is missing."

Where my left breast had once been, there was a huge body depression with drains in it. The area was bloody with pockets of puss everywhere.

"So this is what my truth looks like," I thought. "I hate truth. The truth is hurtful, painful, and ugly. God please, tell me my body will not look like this for the rest of my life. Please, God. Please!"

Gasping for breath. Then quiet. But I wanted to scream.

Dr. Stubbe said nothing but was especially gentle as she tended the wound. She then bandaged the incision again.

I had always been taught not to show anger. Anger was a bad emotion, especially for women. I swallowed deeply. I was swallowing my anger.

Before leaving, the doctor reminded me that recovery time for a skin graft can be quite long. She handed me a pamphlet about grafts. I read, "Most skin grafts are successful, but in some cases do not heal well and require repeat grafting." I began sobbing. I could simply not help myself.

Dr. Stubbe realized I needed to calm down and said to the nurse next to her, "It is obvious that Kay is really upset by all this. Let's get her started on Valium."

Her final comment to me was, "I will need to change the bandage again in a few days. Next time I plan to bring some students along. They need experience treating a mastectomy surgical incision. I just wanted to prepare you for this." I nodded my head but did not really hear what she said.

They left the room, but I had to stay and come to terms with the "new" Kay and my new life. At this point, all I could think of was simply getting home. It became an obsession. I forced myself to believe the familiar trappings of home would make things better.

About day five after surgery, I began having visitors other than my parents and Bill. I so appreciated their visits and their kindnesses. My parents also brought my boys to see me. Seeing the beautiful faces of my Chrissy and Timmy was the **biggest cheer me up I had**. I also began a hospital journal, writing daily entries about my journey with cancer. I desperately needed to keep as busy as possible.

As promised, Doctor Stubbe came back to change my bandages accompanied by three medical students. Stubbe pointed to various parts of the incision, carrying on a conversation describing in detail her surgical procedure. She also explained why she decided to utilize this particular technique.

I was very uncomfortable during this little medical lesson though I did not know why. To Stubbe and her interns, I felt I was not really there. I was a cadaver they were all ogling.

I know no harm was meant, but for me the experience was awful! "Oh, my God," I thought, "I do not believe this is happening." I wanted to shout at all of them, Get out. Have some respect for me. I am not an animal in the zoo. Don't you understand how I feel?

Evidently they did not understand.

I started sobbing and could not stop. Everyone was surprised I was crying, including me. The medical lesson ended. I was given Valium.

My last week in the hospital I experienced what I would call a spiritual encounter. It happened right before I met my oncologist, Dr. Richard Cooper.

I was awakened at 5 AM. The nurse simply said, "Dr. Cooper is coming, and we must get ready for him." When she saw the look of puzzlement on my face, she continued, "This is the first day of your chemotherapy. Dr. Cooper is your oncologist. You will like him. He is doing great work treating cancer and saving lives."

The nurse helped get me up in my hospital bed and brought me a comb for my hair. She wanted everything to be in place before he arrived.

I closed my eyes and said a quick prayer, "Dear God, I am calling to you, asking that the chemo I will be receiving will help me – that it will heal me. Please let me know that you have heard my prayer. I need validation that you are with me, because if you are, I believe I will be able to make it through all this. So right now do *something* that will let me know you are here."

A feeling of calm, of peace, suddenly came over me. It was similar to the amazing peace I had felt a number of years ago before I had emergency surgery for an ectopic pregnancy rupture. I smiled as I thought back on that unforgettable experience. The calming energy immersed every part of my body and mind. Suddenly I knew I could recover from cancer.

A Bible verse came to mind from the book of Philippians: *"And the peace of God, which passes all understanding, shall keep your hearts and minds."* I later found out the exact chapter and verse, Philippians 4:7.

I said a quick, "Thank you, God." When Dr. Cooper came into my room, I was calm and upbeat. Though the feeling of peace only lasted through the morning, I would think back to that magical moment during some of the really bad times ahead. It would help.

Dr. Cooper explained the treatment protocol. He said I would receive injections in the hospital for the next seven days. From that point on I would take daily pills and have chemo injections administered once a week for nine months.

He exuded confidence as he shared information about Cooper's Cocktail, his unique combination of chemotherapy drugs. He asked me if I was ready to begin treatment. I responded with a bold, "Yes." I felt like Caesar crossing the Rubicon River. Iacta Alea Est! The die is cast!

For the next week, my day began with a chemo injection. Initially, my reaction was feeling extremely tired and sleepy. As time passed, I would also experience nausea, sometimes quite severe.

## Chapter Six
### Home, At Last!

*Great music, I am convinced of it, always comes from the heart. Music created with technologies only, is not worth the paper it is written on.*
Maurice Ravel

At last, after two weeks in the hospital, the big day arrived. My family had been preparing for my homecoming for some time, trying their best to make it special for me. Mom and Dad had bought me a beautiful light blue robe for the occasion. It was feminine and lovely – just what I needed.

I was thrilled that Bill was part of the homecoming party. He had taken time off work to help escort me home. He also brought me one dozen beautiful red roses as a coming home gift. They would look lovely on our dining room table and serve as a reminder that things were on an upswing for the Johnson family.

Finally, the meal that Mom prepared was scrumptious -- all my favorite foods: a delicious beef stew, a healthy lettuce salad, and for dessert, her famous pistachio cake. It felt so good to be back home again -- at least for the first night.

But overall, coming home was not the panacea I had hoped. My condition didn't change. A cancer victim and her therapy treatments simply changed locations.

Since I was quite limited in what I could do, my parents decided to stay an additional six weeks to help me get on my feet again. We were all happy that they were extending their stay.

"What in the world would I do without mom and dad," I thought, feeling such gratitude.

My husband could now get back on his regular schedule and no longer needed to visit me at the hospital at the end of his workday. I remember thinking, "This would certainly make Bill happy."

Bill and I needed to have a heart to heart conversation about my cancer and our future. I knew it was possible I might die. I needed to have the *death* conversation with my family, too. However, no one in the family could even say the word *cancer*, let alone talk about the "what ifs" of this debilitating, often fatal disease.

Mom, who usually loved our mother/daughter conversations, finally agreed to have a *serious* talk. She sat down in the comfortable chair beside my bed. I looked at her and said, "Mom, it is so important for me to be able to talk to you about issues so troubling to me now. You probably even know what is most on my mind. I want to talk about Tim and Chris and the possibility of my death. Basically, what everyone would do if that happened?"

That was as far as I got. Mom jumped up from her chair, "This conversation about death does not need to take place – now or ever," she said. "You are going to get well. Do you hear me, Katie? Do you hear me? Since that is what will happen, why in the world would I want to talk about your death? I simply will not do it. End of conversation. I love you so much, my dear daughter, as does dad. You upset us when you bring up these negative things. So please do not do it again."

My mouth dropped. She was out of my room before I could even say, "Mom." I stared off into space for quite some time. I felt completely alone.

As the days progressed, I became more aware of the severity of my situation. The day my hair began falling out, I was showering. As water from the shower hit my head, huge bunches of hair started coming from my scalp, flowed over my body, and finally rested in the shower drain. There was so much hair it actually plugged the drain, and the floor of the shower stall filled with water.

I called out to my mom, "Mom, Mom, please help me. Please help me." Mom ran up the stairs to discover the reason for my panic.

She looked at me with such compassion and gently said, "Katie, come out of the shower, throw on a robe, and we will talk."

To be truthful I do not remember what we talked about, but I do remember putting on my new blue bathrobe, taking a Valium, and going to bed.

When Bill returned home from work that night, he was visibly upset by my loss of hair. I knew I looked very strange bald. Now that I had no hair, I discovered I had a fairly large bluish-black birthmark on the back of my head. It was not a pretty sight.

As he was eyeing my new look, I said to him, "Mom is going out shopping tomorrow to get me some head coverings. Believe it or not, they actually look quite fashionable, coming in a variety of colors." A few tears appeared in my eyes.

Bill blurted out, "Please do not cry, Katie. It drives me crazy. What about me?" So much sadness and fear were in his voice. I had never seen him like this.

"You must know this has been hard on me, too," he continued. "We were both upset by hearing you could not get pregnant again – right? I will not be able to have the daughter I always wanted. That is certainly a downer, but you don't see me crying all the time. Just get over it, okay," he said firmly?

He stormed out of the room. I was shocked at his outburst.

My doctors were adamant that I not get pregnant again. They were afraid pregnancy would bring on a reoccurrence of cancer. When Bill first heard this, he was extremely disappointed. That is understandable. However, his comment was hurtful, and I felt not warranted.

It's funny, looking back on this today, I think I expected Bill to behave perfectly, even though I was not able to. My expectations were just too high for him – and for me. I had so much to learn about relationships.

I also felt a lot of anger toward him. This surprised me because the anger was intense. I was embarrassed by these strong feelings and confused. Confused because so much was happening inside of me I did not understand.

The confusion I dealt with daily increased my depression. Though most cancer patients experience unhappy, sad moments, I was developing a Five-star depression. I am an Aquarian, outgoing, friendly, and excited about possibilities in life. I became a recluse – not wanting to see anyone except my family and sometimes not even them.

My kids were an exception. I always loved being with them. Even when I was bedfast, I built in times each day where we could read stories and play simple games, or they would just play in my bedroom. Sometimes Mom would join us. This was always the best part of my day – the very best part.

They were so full of life, exploring every avenue of possibility in their small worlds. I wanted to be a good mother for them. But my growing depression was making that harder and harder.

I had this overwhelming feeling of lethargy, lacking any kind of motivation. I seemed to be tired all of the time. Life held no excitement for me. I realized how devastating depression can be. I had never felt like this before.

One day Mom asked me to get our mail. But just going outside was more than I could handle. What if a neighbor saw me? Or even worse wanted to talk with me about my breast cancer. I told Mom I just could not do it. I absolutely could not get our mail. I burst into tears. Mom got the mail. I took a Valium and went to bed.

Daily bathing and dressing were awful ordeals. In fact, these two necessary activities provoked buckets of tears for nearly six weeks. Each time I showered I was forced to confront my puss-filled breast incision, missing left breast, and scary wound on my right thigh from the skin graft. When I dried myself with a towel, I had to be careful not to harm both incisions. I prayed they would heal soon. It would take nearly five months for that to happen.

Getting dressed was even more of an ordeal. Since my incision had not yet healed, I was unable to wear a prosthesis or bra. Without the prosthesis, I looked strange. Whether I wore a blouse, sweater, or robe – whatever I wore -- the left side of my chest looked funny. I tried my best to dress without ever looking in the mirror. In fact, I had dad remove the wall mirror from our bedroom. That helped.

At this time, I was also having trouble with the physical therapy I needed to do to strengthen my left arm. My rehab exercises were intended to take the small amount of muscle still left in my arm and stretch it. You can imagine how painful these "stretching" exercises actually were.

I remember one particular morning -- and will forever since it involved my father. I was doing my physical therapy -- specifically the fingers up the wall exercise. On this day, the pain was just too great. My fingers could not progress higher on our bedroom wall.

I found myself feeling so much anger that I had to do all these exercises. It was not fun and too hard – too painful. I was sick of it all. Really sick of everything!

Dad's timing was not good on that day. He just happened to be walking past my room as I was feeling ready to explode in anger. He saw me, popped his head into my room, and said cheerfully, "So my lovely daughter is *walking the wall* again, eh?"

The cheerfulness of his voice was the straw that broke this camel's back. I shouted at him, "The truth is I am about to quit doing this ridiculous exercise. I am sick and tired of it. Dammit, I am so very sick and tired of all my exercises. I just want to quit. I have had it. I cannot do this anymore. I just want to die."

Dad, visibly shaken, walked into the room, looked at me and said, "Today I do not recognize who you are. But you are NOT my daughter. She is an overcomer – not a quitter. She would understand that there are so many people in this world who are in so much worse circumstances. I remember two of my friends from World War II coming home without legs. Imagine living like that."

He was definitely on a roll and continued, "My daughter is fortunate to be alive and have two legs and two arms. She also has a family who loves her. She also knows she is fortunate since her cancer was caught at a fairly early stage. We all believe she WILL live. My daughter, Katie, would not act like a spoiled brat. So I will leave and wait for her to return."

Dad then walked out of the bedroom and stayed away from me the rest of the day.

Mom told me a few days later that this day was a tough one for Dad. She said that he broke down and cried later that night, afraid he had been too harsh with me. She said he was upset because he loved me so much, and simply could not bear hearing me say I was quitting -- that I wanted to die. He just could not *bear* it.

I never did this to my father again. Never. I realized I had a lot of anger inside of me, but had to find other ways of dealing with it. Lashing out at my father was NOT the answer to anything.

Since my immune system was low because of chemo, I contracted the flu. Here I was, an invalid now, unable to get out of bed without help and feeling a desperation that was horrible. For five days I stayed in bed and slept.

I now know that most of my depression, extreme nausea, lethargy, and pain were directly related to the powerful chemo drugs I was receiving. You see the 1970s and 1980s were a time when adjuvant chemotherapy became a major part of how to treat cancer. Massive doses of steroids and other toxic drugs were developed and tried out on cancer patients like me.

There was a lot of experimentation going on back then. Research had shown that often cancer metastasizes because all of the cancer cells were not eradicated initially. Adjuvant chemo was created to remedy this problem. But in 1975, this process was still in its infancy, and doses given were extremely high and powerful. I know people who died from the chemo. On the other hand, the chemo could have saved my life.

# Chapter Seven
## The Transforming Miracle of Music

*I often think in music. I live my daydreams
in music. I see my life in terms of music.*
Albert Einstein

My dad was especially concerned with my fragility, lethargy, and deepening depression. He decided something **must** be done, and done now. He believed I was preparing to die. I felt so horrible physically, so drained mentally, and so overwhelmed emotionally that I did, at times, want to die. Living was too hard. I simply did not have the energy to fight anymore.

Knowing my true love for music, Dad and Bill connected our home intercom system to our living room stereo. They began piping music into my upstairs bedroom -- hoping it would be a catalyst to get me more motivated and focused on living.

"How dare they play this music without asking me? Do they really think this will take my pain away? They do not know how terrible I feel," I said to myself. I was *not* happy with Dad's plan.

But within a few days, the music began to have an effect on me. I became a captive, especially to John Denver's beautiful songs.

John's music touched me at a soul level I did not know existed. The beauty of the melodies and lyrics initiated the reawakening of a string of emotions. A horrible and deeply ingrained sadness was the first to come up for recognition and review.

I found myself breaking into tears constantly – sobbing so hard there was a rawness to it. The pain was like an open wound -- just like the wound left by the removal of my breast – open and ugly.

I even considered not listening to Denver's music anymore, wondering if all of this crying was good for me. Yet this uncertainty changed. Soon I gained an inner assurance that listening to John's music was absolutely the right thing to do.

It was my gut -- my intuition telling me this. Music would help me heal. It would take time, but it would happen. Music would be my springboard to healing and understanding. I just needed to hang in there and not abort the process.

This was a breakthrough moment. Not that everything was easy going now, far from it. I still experienced frustrating and depressing days, but something was changing deep inside of me. I could feel it.

One day I had a mystical experience that would forever change the way I perceived God. I had been feeling anxious and helpless since early morning. I called out to God, "Help me understand why all this is happening. Help me, God. Help me."

Suddenly a feeling of total peace infused my being. I intuitively knew my next step in understanding would be found in Scripture. I rushed over to the bookcase in my room and grabbed my Bible. I clasped it reverently to my heart as if I was taking this Precious Scripture into the love part of me. I then dropped my Bible on my bed, letting it open on its own. As I looked down, I read:

> And when he was demanded of the Pharisees,
> when the kingdom of God should come,
> he answered them and said,
> **The kingdom of God cometh
> not with observation:
> Neither shall they say, Lo here! or, lo there!
> For, behold, <u>the kingdom of God is
> within you.</u>** Luke 17:20, 21 (KJV)

In the twinkling of an eye, I realized I am here on this planet, in this lifetime, to nurture that Divine part of me -- the Christ within me.

My mouth dropped; my eyes widened; my heart raced. I felt as if I had been hit by a bolt of lightning. I whispered to myself, "Wow! So the Kingdom of God is within a person. I have been looking for this Kingdom in the wrong place. But now I get it. I really get it."

Many of the eastern philosophers spoke of the light that resides within us. They, too, say God is found on the inside, deep within oneself. Most of us have disconnected from that source of light – that source of wisdom and guidance.

I immediately thought of a line from Denver's song, "Summer," where he says we are not only connected to each other but to everything in our world. He believes we are a part of everything out there.

I remembered a church song I had been singing for some time now – *"We are One in the Spirit, we are One in the Lord. And we pray that all unity may one day be restored."* I had not realized before how very powerful those lyrics were. They are saying the same thing -- that our reality is *Oneness*. Spiritually we are One. We are from the same source, and we are all part of that source.

Believing this would mean that what I do and what I say is important because of my connection to all others. So when I think dark, negative, demeaning thoughts, these very thoughts are having a negative effect on others in my world. It is better to think positive, uplifting thoughts and help others with my positive energy.

This would also be true of my behavior. If I act in ways that are helpful to myself and others, I model a positive behavior that others may follow. If I perform demeaning, hurtful acts, others might model that, as well. So I need to model the *best behavior* for others to see and emulate. "Wow," I said to myself, "I am more powerful than I ever thought possible."

A few weeks later I had another epiphany experience. It was still winter, but the sun was shining brightly. I said to myself upon waking, "What a beautiful sunny day it is. I do believe that spring will be here soon."

My father had already put on some music. The song playing over the intercom was Denver's "Rhymes and Reasons." Though I had heard this song many times during the past few days, on this particular day it was like God was talking directly to me – connecting to me – through John's music.

As I listened, I felt God saying to me, "My dear, Kay there is so much sadness and fear within you right now – just like John talks about in his song. I want you to see and feel these emotions. Know they are there. They are inside of you. But I am here too, and my power is *greater* than the emotions. You can be healed of this negative emotional takeover. Just trust me."

Suddenly my room filled with a vibrant light. It was shining down on me -- entering my body. I was receiving a powerful Light transfusion and being changed by it. I could feel it.

Suddenly, I absolutely knew the KEY to my recovery was acceptance of my situation – not fighting against it. I must accept I had cancer, had lost my breast forever, and was currently on a chemo regime. Acceptance of my situation would start a whole chain of events that would eventually end with me hopefully recovering from breast cancer.

I was at a major life crossroad. I needed to determine how I was going to live the rest of my life – right now! Would I remain fearful, angry, and scared? Or would I step forward courageously into a future that was unknown? One thing I knew for sure. I would *never* be alone in my new life. God was with me in my *Walk of Faith, Hope, and Love*.

At that moment, I made the decision that would determine my future. **I chose life**. Whether it was life for six weeks or fifty years – I was not sure, but I absolutely knew I wanted to LIVE!

It was time to come out of the darkness – to come out of my cellar of despair – **to begin ascending**! For the second time in my life, I felt like Caesar crossing the Rubicon River. Iacta Alea Est! The die is cast!

Music continued to be my constant companion. It spoke to me facilitating the healing of my mind, body, and spirit.

I concentrated on listening to specific kinds of music, uplifting and inspiring music that helped me transcend the fear and doubt still lurking in shadowy parts of my subconscious. I loved hearing music that reinforced my growing faith in a God of Love who wanted nothing better than to have his children – his Sons and Daughters -- help Him create a beautiful world of freedom and justice.

Church hymns were especially helpful. "Be Still My Soul," "In the Garden," and "How Great Thou Art" bolstered me up. They made me believe in myself as well as my God.

Classical pieces like Beethoven's 5th and 6th symphonies were magnificent, as were the 40th and 41st symphonies of Mozart. I remember dancing around the house while listening to Mozart's, "Jupiter." I simply adored it.

If I were feeling a lack of confidence, I would put on "Pomp and Circumstance" by Sir Edward Elgar. When listening to this elegant and confidence building piece of music, I marched around like I was marching at a graduation or college convocation. It was like I had something to celebrate. As I did this little exercise, I found myself *feeling* regal and assured. Music can do that to us. It can help us feel the very energies and vibrations it is sending forth.

Finally, John Denver's "Sweet Surrender" was extremely helpful and uplifting. *Surrender* does not mean being passive and doing nothing. It does not allow you to simply put up with whatever situation you find yourself in. It is not about being lazy or indifferent. It *is* about yielding to, rather than opposing, the flow of life. It *is* about stopping one's resistance to what is true and making life work for the *best* in spite of the challenges encountered.

Listening to "Sweet Surrender" on my 8 track tapes, I would sing along with John. When my left arm healed, I played guitar and sang solo. I must have sung the last line in "Sweet Surrender" a hundred times. The lyric is saying that my life is worth living, and I want to live it, not have it end. When I sang this last line, I felt I was telling the Universe that I want to live my life! I do not want to die!

In addition, one powerful Scripture verse became my mantra. I repeated it over and over. "I can do all things through Christ who strengthens me" (Philippians 4: 13). When I say repeated it over and over, I mean it. I recited this verse when doing physical therapy and household chores, when friends visited, when nervous about people seeing me with no hair, or when feeling depressed and afraid. My faith increased and slowly my condition improved physically, mentally, and emotionally.

## Chapter Eight
## Understanding the Healing Properties of Dreams

*Music is the shorthand of emotion.*
Leo Tolstoy

Something else quite important to my spiritual growth happened around this time. I started having a recurring dream. Dreams were always important to me, but in 1975, they were especially so.

Repetitive dreams reveal valuable information by pointing out unresolved situations in your life. The dream is an urgent message residing in your unconscious mind, demanding that you confront the unsettled issue and resolve it.

I want to share a specific dream because it was one of the most important of my life. I also knew it was connected to my healing.

In this dream, I am addressed as Mabel Kay, the name I was called the first seventeen years of my life. I was named after my paternal grandmother, Mabel Burgher. When I was seventeen, my father received a job promotion and the family moved to Peru, Indiana. I had never liked my first name, Mabel, and thought this would be the perfect time to drop the Mabel and go by my middle name Kay. I did this, becoming Kay Burgher, rather than Mabel Kay Burgher.

In the dream, I am 32 years old, which is the age I was when I had breast cancer. The setting is my grandmother's home in

Moberly, Missouri, where I lived the first four years of my life. I am sitting in my grandmother's living room with ten to twelve of my relatives – all of us in functional but not very comfortable straight-backed chairs.

I know all the people sitting with me are related to me in some way but I do not recognize any of them. I intuitively know these relatives are genealogically on the Burgher side of the family, my dad's side. The living room is dark even though it is daylight outside. We are all sitting quietly, staring straight ahead. It is like we are dead; no one is moving.

As I sit there, I begin to feel I cannot breathe. It is awful. I believe I will die if I stay in this room. I stand up and say to the group, "I cannot stay here any longer. It is suffocating. I must get out. I must leave."

As I finish speaking, this group of people suddenly change into ghostly figures. They send out a powerful negative energy, which entraps me and keeps me from leaving. Their energy pulls me back down into my chair. They speak, "You cannot leave. You simply cannot leave, Mabel Kay. We will not let you."

I sit down again but feel quite depressed. I realize if I want to live and not be suffocated, I must leave. I stand and speak "I must leave now or I will die. I cannot stand it. This environment is very disturbing and depressing."

The entire group is angry. Their faces become demon-like. "You cannot leave us, do you hear," they order. "You must stay. You do not have a choice."

Their energy is so strong I am overwhelmed. Forced back into my chair once again, I realize I am a captive, possibly forever.

It is more difficult for me to breathe. I cannot tolerate my situation. I stand up, yet again, and say, "I must leave and I will leave, now."

My captors use all their power to keep me from leaving. "You cannot leave, Mabel Kay, we will not let you!" They become devilish and determined. If I try to leave, I know I will be hurt.

Suddenly, I have a powerful thought. **Jesus Christ is with me**! A Bible verse is infused in my mind. "I can do all things through Christ who strengthens me."

I stand up once again. This time, I am standing straight and tall. I feel Jesus by my side. I start walking toward the front door. The goulish figures are grabbing at me trying to pull me back. They are determined to force me into my chair. It is now like a scene from a horror movie. However, I realize my will is stronger than theirs; I have Christ in me.

I continue walking toward the door. Within seconds, I am standing in front of it. I grab the doorknob, turn it, and step outside into the brilliant sunlight. It is so bright, so beautiful. I realize this amazing Light – this sunlight or *Light of the Son* was there all the time. I simply needed to get over my fear and escape from my past forever.

Once outside, I see my small boys, Tim and Chris. They are standing in the sunshine waiting for me.

I thought, "Nothing can separate me from the Love of God." (Romans 8:38). I say to myself, "I know absolutely nothing can separate me from God's amazing and powerful love."

It was evident what this dream was saying. I needed to leave old, outdated family conditionings and outgrown patterns of behavior, not only from my current life but from past lives as well. This was my opportunity to become a brand new person – to open the door to a whole new beginning – to walk in the Light.

I had been raised to be the perfect lady in appearance and manners; however, I was also dependent on men to take care of me. I allowed them to control me and determine my future.

That had to change. I had to change. If I did not do this, I would suffocate. I would die.

I had this dream many times over the next year. Then suddenly, it stopped. I knew I had internalized what I needed to learn.

About a month before my chemo ended, I realized something I had not wanted to acknowledge before. I was becoming addicted to Valium. I had been invited to an all girls' dinner at my BEST friend Barbara Mazur's. Though I was feeling great, I told myself I probably needed to take a Valium – just in case I might need it later. I realized I was behaving in an addictive way.

The next time I saw Dr. Cooper I addressed this issue. He believed I no longer needed this drug, but said if I found I did need it, he would prescribe it again. He gave me a plan for getting off of it which I followed. Within a short time, I no longer took Valium. I was less tired and had more energy.

## Chapter Nine
## John Denver and I Connect

*I would teach children music, physics,
and philosophy; but most importantly
music, for the patterns in music and all
the arts are the keys to learning.*
Plato

After my chemo treatments ended, I decided to write John Denver a letter. I just had to let him know that his music was instrumental in getting me out of depression and helping me heal.

Two weeks after posting it, John's secretary, Peggy Johnston, called to let me know John wanted to talk with me. She said he would call in two days around 11:00 AM. "Be expecting the call," Peggy said, ending the conversation.

After I hung up, I literally ran around our house singing, "John Denver will be calling. John Denver will be calling."

Timmy was at a friend's house. However, Chrissy was home and followed me as I ran around. He finally got my attention saying, "Mommy, are you okay?"

"Yes, Chrissy, I am wonderful, absolutely wonderful."

Chrissy broke into a big smile. He looked so precious, I swooped him up into my arms, and together we danced around the house singing our little Denver ditty. After a few minutes of this exuberance, we stopped, looked at each other, and broke into laughter. This was such a memorable morning, and I was so delighted that I could share my excitement with my sweet son.

On the morning John was to call, my boys and I were up and dressed early. There were, at least, five phone calls prior to John's. This was hilarious since all of the calls were from good friends wanting to know if John had called me yet.

Each time the phone rang, Chrissy would excitedly say, "Mom, maybe this is John Denver." Both of my boys had heard John's music and knew most of the words to his songs as well as I did. They completely understood how excited I was to be able to talk to him.

"Mommy, you know I really like John Denver, too," Timmy said. "I think I like his song, 'Country Roads', best of all. Would you tell John Denver that for me?"

I picked up this precious child and said, "Yes, Timmy, I will tell John. In fact, maybe you can tell him yourself. Would you like that?"

He responded, a bit shyly, "No, mom it's okay, you just tell him." I promised him I would.

When the phone rang the sixth time, Chrissy said more emphatically, "Mom, I think it is John Denver this time."

I took a deep breath, wondering if my boys could hear my pounding heart. I realized my hands were shaking. I said a quick prayer, "Dear God, you know how terribly excited I am. Please help me say what is in my heart. I really want to get it right today."

I continued to make myself breathe slowly and sort of half skipped and half walked to the phone. I picked up the receiver and nervously said, "Hello."

I then heard *the* voice -- the voice I had laughed with, cried with, and now truly loved. I heard the voice of my new friend, John Denver, say, "Hello, is this Kay?"

I responded eagerly "Yes, it is Kay."

And from the phone receiver, "Kay, this is John Denver calling. It is good to speak with you. It gives me a chance to let you know how happy I am that the music worked for you. That it helped you during your battle with cancer. That is really far out."

Tears filled my eyes; my throat seemed to close; yet, I knew I had to pull myself together, so I could talk. But hearing his voice was such an emotional experience for me.

To me, John seemed like family now. He had been with me during the most challenging time of my life. Through the pain, the sadness, the fear, the laughter, the joy; John was there through it all.

He continued, "You know you said in your letter that my music was magic for you. I really liked that thought. I think music can be magic, too. I know you especially like my songs 'Sweet Surrender' and 'Rhymes and Reasons.' I'd be interested in knowing why those songs helped you in your recovery?"

I told him about the very first time I heard the lyrics and music to "Sweet Surrender." I felt lost and alone, no doubt about that at all.

"But, John," I said, "your lyrics went on to describe what you needed to do during the lost, lonely times. You needed to *surrender* – surrender to going with the flow of life – not fighting against it. That is THE key," I said, "the key for sure."

"Plus, your music seemed to move in a forward direction," I continued. "It was beautiful. It seemed to flow. There were no obstacles to stop those gorgeous sounds. No dissonant sounds or abrupt changes of directions. Just a beautiful flow, like *surrendering*," I continued.

I went on to share more about his music's therapeutic powers. Then, I changed the topic, "You know, John, one of your new songs, 'Looking to Space,' had the same effect. I was hooked immediately. I, too, am looking for answers to why I am here, and what is my purpose?"

"Well", said John, "we really are kindred spirits. You know I received Werner Erhard's EST training, and the song you like so much I dedicated to him and everyone in EST."

I did know this. Werner Erhard, now a friend of his, conceived of EST or Erhard's Seminars Training in the mid-1970s. The training consisted of two week-long workshops where personal transformation and taking responsibility for one's life was the focus for discussion and activities.

"I am happy to know you like my new song," John responded.

"I do like it, very much," I said enthusiastically, "but the song I sing most is your beautiful 'Sweet Surrender'."

"I am happy to hear that Kay." I could tell by the sound of his voice he was smiling.

I suddenly remembered what Timmy had asked me to tell John, "By the way, both of my little guys, Chrissy, and Timmy, like your music almost as much as I do. Timmy wants me to tell you how much he likes 'Country Roads.' In fact, it is his favorite."

I then held the phone to Timmy's ear, so he could hear John's reply.

"Far out," responded an enthusiastic Denver, "Tell, Timmy I said Far Out." Hearing John's response, Timmy broke into the sun-shiniest smile I had ever seen. My little boy was delighted.

John and I talked for nearly twenty-five minutes. He shared his deep belief that the music he writes is not really his but rather everyone's. He's just the person – or in his words -- the *"instrument who writes it down."* I found his philosophy inspiring.

As we said our good-byes, he promised when he performed in Buffalo again, he would send me a backstage pass, so we could meet. I heard him tell Peggy to put that on his Buffalo calendar. I was ecstatic.

I broke into a big smile and said, "It just doesn't get any better than this." But it did get even better. I met him!

When John next performed in Buffalo, New York, we met after his concert! Thank goodness I had the foresight to bring a camera.

*Meeting John Denver*

# Chapter Ten
## My Early Years And Music

*There is no feeling, except the extremes of fear
and grief that does not find relief in music.*
George Eliot

My conversation with John made me realize it was time to become proactive and take the next step in my new life. I made this decision all on my own!

I was certain I wanted to share my story with other cancer patients as well as medical personnel. Most important, I wanted my presentation to focus on the role *music* played in my recovery and healing.

The truth is music was *always* a big part of my life, from the very beginning. You might even say I entered the world surrounded by love and music.

Born in February of 1943, the early years of my life were spent in the stately, two-story, brick home of my charismatic grandparents, Mabel and Rex Burgher. Living in Moberly, Missouri was such a blessing, and I have come to cherish the many benefits of growing up in a small town.

Since the country was just coming out of the Great

Depression, we felt fortunate to be living in such a large house. We actually had four bedrooms in the upstairs, one of which grandma rented out to a border, Elvergia Denning, a librarian at our local Junior College.

My grandparents were true music lovers who in the nineteen thirties invested in a beautiful, black, Wurlitzer baby grand piano. They had saved for many years to be able to afford it. The moment it arrived my grandfather sat down on the bench and began playing one of his favorite hymns. He and grandma knew their decision was a wise one. Both of these dear people believed having music in the house was a *necessity*—every bit as important as food. A house without music was a house without joy, and they were determined to have a joyful house.

Soon after the piano arrived their only daughter, my Aunt Billie Ruth, began taking piano lessons, eventually becoming an accomplished pianist. Grandpa also loved playing the six or seven hymns he knew. Sometimes he would sit at the piano for hours, deeply engrossed in creating unique and pretty little tunes that he would put words to. The Burgher baby grand was never lonely but had regular visitors; each of whom found great joy in playing it.

At the end of each day, after the dinner dishes were washed and put away, the family would gather in the spacious living room for a little family musicale. Billie Ruth, or Aunt Bill as I called her, would be at the piano. Grandpa, who I lovingly named *Gampa* -- my feeble attempt at saying grandpa -- would be standing by her side, leading our little sing-a-long. Grandma would be sitting in her black wooden rocker with me in her lap enjoying the festivities immensely.

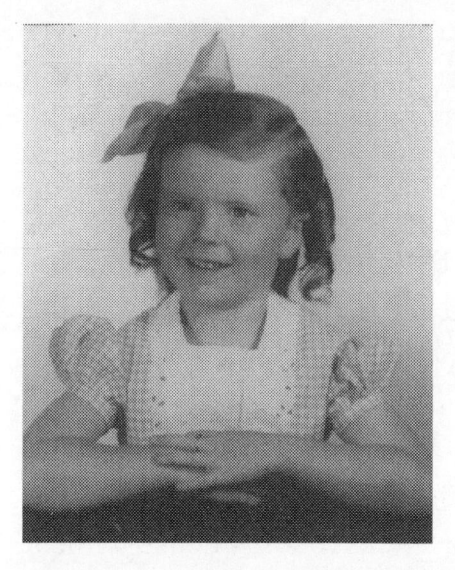

Gampa seemed quite comfortable in the position of leader and would begin the evening by saying, "All right, family, are you ready to sing?"

We would all say politely, "Yes, we are."

That little opening led to thirty-five or more minutes of musical singing. Gampa would start off with a really upbeat song like, "Oh You, Beautiful Doll," and we would go from there.

When I turned three, I began taking both tap and ballet lessons. That same year I also began officially singing and dancing for the public. Mom would take me to numerous talent shows in the Randolph County area where I would sing my little heart out competing for prizes with other talent show contestants.

I have been told I was a red-headed version of Miss Shirley Temple, a popular child star of the era. My bright, red hair was curled in ringlets like Shirley's. We were also about the same size.

I was a real hit at these talent contests, often placing first. Usually, that meant I would come home with a brand new ten-dollar bill and a blue ribbon. If I came in second, the money would be less, only five dollars -- and the ribbon, pink. I remember one talent show in Macon, Missouri, where first prize was a brand new twenty-dollar bill, a lot of money back then. I was thrilled to win this, as I knew the money would help my family.

Shortly after turning five, I began taking piano lessons. Playing piano was one of the great loves of my life. I was so excited when my parents told me I could finally begin. It seemed to me I had been waiting forever.

I would continue my lessons until I was seventeen. By that time, I was a pretty good pianist and loved playing the dramatic classical music of Mozart, Beethoven, Rachmaninoff, Chopin, and Mendelssohn

I became organist at our First Baptist Church when I was only twelve. This was quite an accomplishment, delighting my dear Gampa. I was organist there for just over five years and came to cherish this unique opportunity.

I remember walking over to our church after school to practice. I had the whole sanctuary to myself and could explore all the different combinations of sounds from our huge Wurlitzer pipe organ. It was such a wonderful time in my life. Being surrounded almost daily by organ music was my idea of heaven.

I would often continue my practice until it was dark outside or till around 5:30 PM if it were winter. There was something almost mystical about playing in the empty sanctuary with darkness coming on. I was not the least bit frightened.

A few of my friends, however, thought I must be crazy to like playing the organ in the dark. But the experiences I found so fascinating and enjoyable were sometimes not the same as my classmates.

Throughout my life, I would continue playing the organ for churches in Western New York. My last full-time organ position was at the North Park Presbyterian Church in Buffalo from 1984 to 1990.

From 1965 to 1970 I was an elementary teacher at St. Leo's Parochial School in Buffalo. In the evenings, I taught myself how to play the guitar, so I could accompany myself whenever I sang for Mass or other events. I even taught some of my elementary students how to play the guitar.

Throughout my life, I taught both piano and guitar lessons to students of all ages. I loved putting on student recitals at various churches in the area, as these presentations provided a platform that allowed my students to *shine*.

Writing songs was also something I thoroughly enjoyed. Many of my original compositions were simple hymn-like melodies which I could then use as a Sunday organ or piano prelude. So, as you can see, music played a major role in my life from the time I was quite small.

As a child, I realized music could affect my emotions. I was **always very sensitive** and would get quite upset over argumentative exchanges and loud, dissonant sounds. I remember one day when I was ten overhearing a family argument. My parents did not realize I was listening. Their angry words were extremely upsetting to me. I found myself feeling anxious and depressed.

I thought Pachelbel's "Canon in D" might help my beleaguered spirit. As I played the piece, the rhythmic pattern and soothing sound affected me emotionally. It calmed me down. I continued playing and calmed down even more. It seemed magical.

I discovered "Moonlight Sonata" by Beethoven was another emotionally calming piece. "My goodness," I said, "music does affect me. I am amazed and delighted to know this now."

Before I was thirty-two, I did not recognize how STRONGLY music connected to emotions. My experience with cancer, and especially the depression I experienced because of my cancer, would be the catalyst for my new awareness of the actual *clout* of music.

# Chapter Eleven
## How the Ancients Viewed Music

*Music in the soul can be heard by the universe.*
Lao Tzu

The effects of music, both positive and negative have been debated for centuries. In Plato's **Republic** explicit mention is made of the powers of music to build character, self-control, peacefulness, and social order; or to contribute to alienation, discontent, and subversion of the social order. Plato argued that a philosopher king should promote certain kinds of music and censor others.

He observed music's ability to reinforce particular emotions on an unsuspecting society when he said, "Any musical innovation is full of danger to the whole state, and ought to be prohibited. When modes of music change, the fundamental laws of the state always change with them."

This great philosopher further explained how music played an important role in the *moral decline* of ancient Greece: "They were men of genius, but they had no perception of what was just and lawful in music...And by composing licentious works, and adding to them words as licentious, they have inspired the multitude with lawlessness and boldness, and made them fancy that they could judge for themselves about melody and song."

(See the Philosophers Talk Music, Internet http://amazingdiscoveries.org/S-deception-music_philosophers_culture_plato)

Socrates did an extensive study into the effects of music. He, too, recognized its potential as an instrument of indoctrination and character development. "Musical training is a more potent instrument than any other because rhythm and harmony find their way into the inward places of the soul, on which they mightily fasten, imparting grace, and making the soul of him who is rightly educated graceful, or of him who is ill-educated ungraceful," Socrates is quoted as saying.

(See the Philosophers Talk Music, Internet http://amazingdiscoveries.org/S-deception-music_philosophers_culture_plato)

Half way around the globe in China, the great sage Confucius believed there was a correlation between good music and a moral society. He is quoted as saying, "If one should desire to know whether a kingdom is well governed, if its morals are good or bad, the quality of its music will furnish the answer."

According to these philosophers, music's power seemed to lie in the kinds of sounds created by the instruments and the rhythmic patterns used. I believe instrumental and voice sounds create a variety of emotional energies. This energy then reinforces these same emotions within listeners without them even knowing it is happening.

So what are the specific traits or characteristics that determine good or moral music from bad or immoral music? This information is much less clear and gets tricky since imposed censorship is not what freedom is about.

However, since so many enlightened, respected men from antiquity talk about *music's power*, it seems to be fertile ground for continuing exploration and research today.

Even as I write this memoir, studies are taking place at colleges and universities around the world to help determine the truth of all this. I look forward to reading more about music's power because of my own personal experience as I dealt with breast cancer. I can say, unequivocally, that I believe music brought me out of a severe depression and helped me heal.

I learned I needed to pay much more attention to how the music I listened to affected me. Like food, just because we enjoy something does not mean it is good for us. Learning to *discern* whether the music in our lives is a help or a hindrance is important and can facilitate our creation of a more positive and productive life.

## Chapter Twelve
## Volunteering for The American Cancer Society (ACS)

*If one should desire to know whether a kingdom is well governed, if its morals are good or bad, the quality of its music will furnish the answer."*
Confucius

About six months after my phone conversation with John Denver, I began to intuit I needed to share my new spiritual insights via music. I awoke quite early one morning feeling inspired and knowing this was my morning to write a down-to-earth song about life – the ups and downs – the highs and lows. I had seen a beautiful rainbow the day before and knew the song would be based on components of a rainbow – the sunshine and the rain.

I went to my desk, grabbed paper and pencil, and within thirty minutes had penned the words to my song. The melody came even quicker. I believe it was inspired from *on high*.

Dr. Kay Johnson-Gentile

## **IT TAKES BOTH SUNSHINE AND RAIN TO MAKE A RAINBOW**

1. Do you wish your life could
be a whole lot brighter?
Much more sunshine, fewer storms
that soak us through.
But there's a reason for the rain.
Understanding we can gain.
There's a rainbow just around the bend for you.

**Chorus**
It takes both sunshine and rain to make a rainbow.
Both are needed to give off its special hue.
It takes both happiness and sorrow to make living
An experience of growth for me and you.

3. Remember sunshine all the
time would make a desert.
A shower of rain can cleanse a
person make them new.
Trying times are times for trying.
Forget mistakes, stop your sighing
There's a rainbow just around the bend for you.

4. You know each new day brings
another fresh beginning
A chance for making others smile it is true.
Life is not just what you make it
Many times it's how you take it.
There's a rainbow just around the bend for you.

 I loved the song, especially the uplifting message – "There's a Rainbow, just around the bend for you!" Of course, since I was hoping to survive breast cancer, I did want to believe that my rainbow was in reach. And you know what? Singing this positive song helped me believe in that positive outcome even more.

 Contacting the American Cancer Society (ACS) was my next step. I called and volunteered my services, asking to share my own unique story and demonstrate how *music* helped in my recovery. I planned to use some of my newly written music in my program. I could not wait to get started as an ACS speaker.

*Dr. Kay Johnson-Gentile*

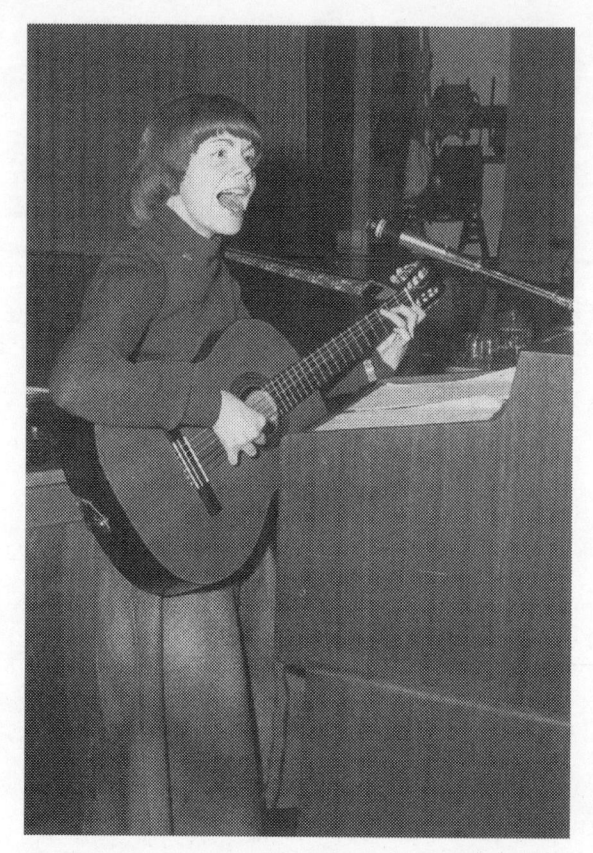

*Perfroming for the American Cancer Society*

The Cancer Society embraced me warmly, and over the next few years, I traveled the United States speaking and singing at ACS meetings, conventions, and to groups of cancer patients and medical personnel. I was even asked to create and direct a volunteer music therapy program for children with cancer. Though initially very nervous about accepting these challenges, I believed God was calling me to do them. Besides, I would not be alone: *"I can do all things through Christ who strengthens me" (Philippians 4:13).*

With the support of the New York State Division of the ACS, dedicated hospital staff and personnel, and a number of wonderful volunteers, our Volunteer Music Therapy Program for Children and Adolescents with Cancer was initiated in the Fall of 1977 at Roswell Park Cancer Institute in Buffalo, New York.

Though I had degrees in Music and Education, I was not a therapist. So before beginning our new venture, I contacted the Chair of the Music Therapy (MT) Department at the State University College at Fredonia. I was hopeful she might be interested in participating, along with MT students from the college.

The Chair thought it was a good idea since it presented opportunities for Fredonia students to do internships at the hospital. The Occupational Therapist at Roswell, Jeanne Mehle, agreed to supervise the Fredonia students. It all worked out like clockwork.

I also enlisted volunteers to work with me in conducting our bi-weekly, hour and a half evening sessions. Jim Totaro, the Rehabilitation Counselor at Roswell, wanted to participate in this part of our program, as did my good friend and Lockport Elementary Music Teacher, Doni Koukal. Before we knew it, we had our program up and running.

As I worked one-on-one with the young people at Roswell, I found myself inspired on a daily basis. This initiated yet another period of intense music writing. I finally decided it was important to have this music available for all families in crisis, as well as for people who just liked positive, upbeat songs.

Next came the creation of my first record album, "Faith, Hope, and Love." A number of talented musicians helped with this endeavor including Tony Gallo, Randy Pesano, Ron Gentile, Jim Palys and Ray Domanski.

*My record album, Faith, Hope, and Love*

When the album was released, we had a *kick-off concert* in Lockport. Since attending concerts was one of the goals of our music program, special invitations were sent to our Roswell kids and parents, as well as Roswell Park staff.

After the concert, I had a chance to talk to all of the people from Roswell. They all told me they were in favor of more concerts.

Shortly after this, I found out John Denver was scheduled to perform in Buffalo again. I thought this would be a great second concert for our MT kids. By contacting some of John's public relations staff, we were able to make this happen. John not only donated tickets to his concert but agreed to meet the kids afterward.

When I announced to the Roswell crew what John had done, everyone was thrilled. After all, John was one of the top celebrities in the USA – and the world for that matter. This was a dream come true for us all.

One of the children in our program called me from her home near New York City to ask if she and her mom could attend John's concert even though she was not currently receiving treatment at Roswell.

"I absolutely adore John Denver and cannot imagine anything better than hearing him sing in person," she said.

"There are two tickets waiting for you and your mom when you arrive. It's great that you and your mom can come. See you soon," I said.

My husband and I arrived at the hospital about two hours before concert time. Though we had already arranged for transporting the children to the concert arena, I wanted to be there early to take care of any last minute problems that might arise. Thankfully, everything went extremely well.

As our little convoy of forty people marched into the arena to find our ground floor seats, we must have been a sight to behold. Besides myself, my husband, and three other volunteers, Roswell's rehab counselor was there, along with three nurses, the occupational therapist, two doctors, and a number of parents. Most important though were the children and adolescents, all of them excited and animated.

As I glanced around the arena, I could see that everyone in our group was positioned so we could all see the stage well. We had about twenty minutes before the concert began. I was trying my best to take it all in. I knew this would be a night I would always remember.

There was the normal pre-show chatter. It was wonderful to see all these children laughing and enjoying themselves. I remember a few of our kids asking me where we would go to meet John after the concert. They wanted to be sure I knew what I was doing – that nothing could foul up their meeting a superstar.

I smiled and told them not to worry, a special escort was coming to where we were and would take us backstage to John after the concert ended. They relaxed after hearing that.

From the first glorious sounds of Lee Holdridge's beautiful arrangements of Denver's tunes I just knew this concert would be spectacular! Lee and John were the *perfect* team, and the music from this unique partnership brought joy to millions of people world-wide.

The first half of the show went by quickly. John invited the audience to sing along with him on many of his songs. I loved watching the kids as they got into the music -- clapping, singing, and swaying their bodies back and forth in rhythm. It was obvious they were having a great time.

But to me, the song that really touched the hearts of these kids was his beautiful "I Want to Live." *I Want to Live* was also the name of John's latest record album, released in November of 1977. The words to this touching song say that kids everywhere want to live, to grow, to explore, and to know - but more than anything else, each child wants to have the chance **to live** their life to the fullest.

When John began singing this touching song, I had a short moment when I was concerned. I wondered if the powerful lyrics would be too much for our Roswell kids. As John continued singing, I perused the faces of our children, and to my great joy, their faces were beaming. Of course, there were tears in our little group, too – from nearly everyone. As the song ended applause from our Roswell cohort was intense.

A number of them jumped to their feet cheering, calling out, "Yes, John," "Way to Go, John," or "We love you, John

Denver!" I thought to myself, you know John is expressing through his music what every one of our kids is feeling – what is in *all of their* hearts. How wonderful to experience this powerful Denver song together!

Tears filled my eyes. I bowed my head and said a prayer that the miracle of tonight would sustain these children through the cold, dark days they would have to face to get cancer free. I knew each of their cancer journeys would not be easy.

When the concert ended, our special escort came to take us backstage to meet John. Everyone was excited and happy. At least for tonight, life seemed *amazing* for these children. As I watched the escort telling the kids what would be happening when they met John, it dawned on me how fortunate I was to be part of all this. *Doing things for others* is where we experience our greatest JOY.

The next thing I knew I heard a cheerful, "Far Out." I chuckled. I certainly knew where that statement came from.

John was in his element – giving hugs and high-fiving – making each child feel so important, so special. I was tremendously moved by this scene, so much so that tears were running down my face. "I absolutely LOVE this talented, caring man," I thought. "It just doesn't get any better than this."

I had a number of amazing nights in my life, but this night is at the top of my *Amazing Nights List*. It was a perfect evening --just perfect.

The two years I coordinated this music program were memorable months filled with triumphs, challenges, and all the intense experiences and interactions one would expect to have when dealing with life and death situations. During this time, I met some of the most *courageous* children, adolescents, and parents I had ever met. I will never forget them.

One of these memorable children was Melissa, a beautiful five-year-old child with the biggest, most expressive eyes I have ever seen. From talking with her parents I learned Melissa was the *perfect* youngster, having a loving, calm temperament. She never gave her folks a moment of concern. When she came down with acute lymphoblastic leukemia (ALL) -- the most common type of cancer in young children --Melissa's entire family was devastated.

I had come to the hospital early, around 10:00 AM, hoping to visit with some of our kids one-on-one before lunch time. My short, 15-minute sing-a-long sessions were quite successful. The kids liked both the singing and personal attention. I was especially looking forward to singing with Melissa. When I met her and her parents a few months ago, we hit it off. She loved our program, especially our sing-a-longs.

As I walked down the hall approaching Melissa's room, I heard a ruckus going on inside. Though I could not see in the room, I was pretty sure it was Melissa who was screaming. This was so unlike her. It sounded as if something horrible was happening, and she was scared.

To be honest, I wanted to skip by this whole scene. It is one thing to do a sing-a-long with a child who is calm and happy, but Melissa was anything but that. I said to myself, "I have absolutely no idea what I would do if I were with Melissa right now. I do not think I should get involved in this." I walked faster. I hoped to get past her room without being seen.

That did not happen. Melissa's mom saw me and came running up to me. In a breathless, agitated voice she said, "Kay, please come back with me to Melissa's room. My daughter is giving us a hard time. Maybe you can help out. I know how much she likes you."

I honestly felt trapped. I didn't want to see Melissa as she was so upset. But I said, "Sure I will come."

As I entered the room, I could see why the child was distressed. It was evident she was having medical treatments or tests involving needles. Melissa hated needles!

The nurse was trying to insert yet another one of those "needles" into this sweet child's bruised little arm and was having trouble finding a place for the insertion. My heart went out to this unhappy child who looked confused, depressed and *trapped*.

When she saw me, she calmed down a bit. She looked at me intently, waiting to hear what I had to say to her. After all, I was her friend, the music lady.

More than anything else I wanted to help Melissa. But how? What could I do? I thought this is probably just how her mother feels.

I had my guitar with me, and said, "Melissa, I can see this is a bad time for you. What if I played something you like on my guitar..."?

That is as far as I got. The screaming began again, only now it was louder. A look of disappointment and anger was on her face, as if what I said hurt her deeply.

Everyone looked at me. I snapped my fingers, hoping I would disappear from the scene. I was still there. Melissa's distress continued.

The nurse, now also quite frustrated, said "Melissa, you must calm down. You know we are trying to help you, not hurt you. Why are you so upset? Please calm down so we can continue your treatment."

Melissa screamed louder.

I said a prayer, silently, "Please help us all, God. Help us to help Melissa. And help me to know what I am to do right now."

As my prayer ended, I picked up my guitar and started strumming very loudly, very angrily a variety of dissonant chords. Responding *in the moment* I started singing, making up my little song as I went along.

> "I DON'T WANT TO BE HERE!
> I WANT TO GO HOME!
> I DON'T WANT TO BE HERE. I
> WANT TO GO HOME.
>
> DOESN'T ANYBODY HEAR ME? ISN'T
> ANYBODY THERE? PLEASE SOMEONE
> HEAR ME. SHOW ME THAT YOU CARE.
>
> I DON'T' WANT TO BE HERE.
> I WANT TO GO HOME.
> I DON'T WANT TO BE HERE. I
> WANT TO GO HOME"

Suddenly, Melissa stopped screaming and looked up at me with those beautiful blue eyes. "I'll sing that song, Kay. I will sing that song," she said. Together Melissa and I sang the song I had just made up -- and sang it with enthusiasm.

Then Melissa's mom said, "I want to sing, too, Kay, because I don't want to be here either. Melissa feels so horrible here because the treatments are so painful to her. I wish I was home, too -- home with my sweet daughter."

The three of us sang the song. There were tears in her mother's eyes, which Melissa saw. Melissa reached out and took hold of her mother's hand.

The nurse, envisioning the whole scene, looked at Melissa and said, "Can I sing the song, too, Melissa? I do not want to be here either since I see how much what I am doing hurts you. I wish I did not have to do these treatments."

Melissa responded, softly, "Yes, you can sing with us."

Now the four of us sang the song with gusto.

All this time, Melissa was calming down more and more. Finally, after about ten minutes of singing, with the adults expressing how badly they all felt about the situation, Melissa was calm and able to get through the necessary tests.

I thought to myself, the reason Melissa calmed down was because the *truth* had finally entered into this little scene. The truth was NO ONE wanted to be here, under these circumstances, making this beautiful child feel so badly. Each of us would prefer being home.

However, right now this is where we all *needed* to be. It was the only way we knew to help this child – to hopefully save her from an early death. For Melissa, she had spoken -- or should I say *sung* her *truth*. That was enough to get her through the challenge of this day. It was enough -- at least for now.

Words cannot describe the compassion and love I developed for the children I worked with at Roswell Park. That compassion also extended to their caring and oft times exhausted parents. Dealing with a child's cancer can be devastating.

I remember another pair of gallant parents standing by their unconscious, dying child; taking her hand, squeezing it, and whispering softly, "This is Mommy, sweetie. Daddy and I are right here beside you. Your teddy bear, Paddy, is here, too. We will all stay right here. You know we love you very much. You are such a joy to us. We just feel so blessed to have you as our beautiful child."

"This is Ruthie, honey, your night nurse. I will be right here for you, too. You know, I think you are a wonderful little girl. I have come to love your beautiful spirit. And your sweet smile has brightened up so many of my nights. You are the best," she haltingly said, as her eyes teared.

"Kay," said the child's mother, would you sing our daughter's favorite song, 'You are My Sunshine?' I think she would like to hear it."

"Yes, I would love to sing this song for my sweet friend," I said picking up my guitar to sing.

As I sang I looked directly at the child, sending the most profound love her way. Often the child's face seemed to relax more, and tension in the brow and eye areas lesson. Seeing this happen was something I would never forget.

How I ever made it through the song without breaking down is something I would *never* understand. I knew the parents were counting on me to do this, and I knew the child loved the song. Possibly that was the reason. Because whenever I was in this situation I was able to come through.

I also believed I received help from *on high*. That is what made the most sense to me.

I gained a new appreciation of the doctors, nurses, aides and all hospital personnel who worked with cancer children. It was evident it took a toll on these competent and dedicated individuals.

This was such a learning time for me. But, after two years I knew I needed to resign. I had seen a world I had not known existed. I was beginning to bring home my deep sadness for these children. It began to have an effect on me and my family.

When I finally resigned, I found myself missing the children I had worked with at Roswell. I made a couple of surprise visits back to the hospital, just to see the kids again. After I left, the music program continued. I was, of course, delighted.

I did pursue my travels with the ACS. Doing this helped me realize how much I enjoyed talking before audiences and telling my cancer story. Then with guitar in hand I would break into song -- singing about the feelings cancer patients and their families experience. The music made my story more powerful – more real.

Doing this also made me feel I was making a contribution -- a contribution to other cancer patients. And anything I could do to make a cancer patient's life a little more pleasant, I wanted to do. The pleasure I received from this work was *immeasurable*.

*Receiving an Award for my work with the ACS*

For this volunteer work, I was selected as *One of Ten Outstanding Young Women of America* for 1977. When I went to Washington, D.C. to receive my award, I met the nine other winners. Getting to know each of them was a highlight. All ten of us also had the great opportunity to have a roundtable discussion with then Vice President, Walter Mondale.

As we were sitting in the White House chatting with Mondale, I remember thinking, "I simply cannot believe I am here. God has blessed me beyond measure. And all this began with breast cancer. Now I am one of ten outstanding young women talking with the Vice President of the United States."

One of John Denver's songs – "It Amazes Me" – popped into my mind. I chuckled. "Far out," I said. "I am just so grateful – so very grateful."

*Meeting Vice President Walter Mondale*

## Chapter Thirteen
### Beginning My Walk of Faith, Hope, and Love

*Where words leave off, music begins.*
Heinrich Heine

Yes, life was falling into place in ways I never imagined possible. Having cancer was like a Great Awakening. I felt so alive and empowered. In addition, a book I had devoured nearly fifteen years before, Betty Friedan's, *The Feminine Mystique*, was about to have a powerful effect on my life.

My next door neighbor, Katie, also gave me a book as a gift. "This book may be helpful to you, Kay. And since you are searching for books with a spiritual message you will like Andersen for sure".

The book, *Three Magic Words*, was written by Uell S. Anderson. The message was perfect for me. Andersen says there is only one creator -- the Universal Mind or God. He says our thinking creates our reality. To change our life, we must change our thoughts. Most of all we need to think in a positive fashion and believe in ourselves. Thinking more in *Yes, I Can* ways takes us far.

Meditation helped in this process. Andersen believed meditation could change the structure of the brain, enhancing and accelerating cognition. It could sharpen our creative capacity allowing us to concentrate and focus more effectively.

Finally, meditation could reduce anxiety and depression. It calms us down, giving us control of our lives.

I decided to put the message of this book into action. I began rising early each morning -- between 4:30 and 5:00 -- to meditate. I would sit still and follow the procedures recommended in the book. Within two weeks I noticed a subtle change taking place within me.

Initially, when I meditated, I had to force myself to get up at 4:30. I was not happy about it. That changed. Though I still set the alarm, when it went off, I could not wait to begin my meditation. Within a month's time, I did not even need an alarm!

Coming out of meditation one morning I felt I was being infused with energy. I knew this energy was Divine – it was from God! I was not at all afraid. I felt very peaceful.

I visualized a very long pathway or trail. Both sides of the path were strewn with majestic trees, gorgeous shrubs, and fragrant multi-colored flowers. The scene was stunning. To make the vision even more spectacular the day was sunny – in a *brilliant* way – like everything was so clear and bright you understood the reason for existence itself!

I realized I had been given the chance to continue my walk – the walk I had begun during my bout with cancer. The walk was symbolic. It represented a sort of *purification and growth process* I needed to go through.

Suddenly, out of nowhere a feeling of darkness passed through my body. It was frightening. I intuitively knew that up ahead the landscape was not lovely, not beautiful. It was dark and scary -- devoid of shrubs, flowers, and trees – devoid of beauty!

"Though your walk begins in beautiful, peaceful surroundings, your journey will require you to traverse scary, desolate areas, as well," a bold, yet kindly voice said. "But – this journey is what you are supposed to do in this lifetime. **It is your life plan, your life purpose."**

"You will be sent the kinds of life experiences you need for spiritual and soul development. **Whatever comes your way is a GIFT**. Think of even the toughest or most painful life situation as a beautiful gift designed to teach you the unique and particular soul lesson you need to learn. Never be afraid. As they *mystics* tell us, this journey will take you **back to the Heart of God."**

"Can you walk this walk?" the voice questioned in a hopeful tone. "Can you continue your journey? **You do have a choice**."

I knew I had to answer now.

Without hesitation I called out, "Yes. **Yes, I *can*** continue my walk, even when it is dark and painful, and I cannot see where I am going. **Yes, I can** do that. Yes!"

"Very well," replied the voice, "I am happy to hear that – very happy. Remember, you are *never* alone. Beings of Light - beautiful angels will be with you always even unto the end of your world."

"Your walk is a **Walk of Faith, Hope, and Love** because you will need all three of these spiritual qualities to make it to the end."

"**Faith** will carry you through when you cannot see the path clearly. It will help you know the trail is still there."

"**Hope** will be your guide when all seems lost. It will keep you going in spite of the darkness and loneliness you encounter along the way."

"**Love**, the greatest of the three, will be the catalyst that provides you with the Heart -- the staying power -- to get through to the end. Be assured continuing to the end will NOT be easy. There will be times when the walk seems just too painful -- you will want to quit. That is when Love will help you stay on the path."

"Faith, Hope, and Love are the keys to completing your walk of Victory -- of Healing. So, are you ready to continue the walk?" the voice asked.

For yet a third time in my life, I felt like Caesar crossing the Rubicon. Iacta Alea Est! The die is cast!

"Yes, I am ready," I said with conviction.

As I came out of this transforming experience, I knew I had to write a song that spoke to the three powerful spiritual qualities of Faith, Hope, and Love. I walked to my desk, snatched up paper and pencil, and within minutes had penned the words to my song. Grabbing my old six-string acoustic guitar, I began plunking out and notating the melody.

I felt connected to the Universe, like I was part of a vast plan of creation. My important though small role was penning the song, *"Faith, Hope, and Love."*

And this is the end of my little narrative, dear readers. But it is not an ending – but a beginning!

Be blessed.

Kay

*Walking the path of Faith, Hope, and Love*

## **FAITH, HOPE, LOVE – THIS IS WHAT I SELL**

1. Each day I live becomes a new adventure.
Adventure is the word I want to use.
My hopes are riding high; My spirits really fly.
My life is up to me and what I choose.
My life is up to me and what I choose.
It's up to me and what I choose.

### CHORUS
Cause I'm alive and feeling free.
And I'm happy to be me.
And I hope you're happy to be you as well.
Oh, Golly Gee, life's so special don't you see.
Faith, Hope, Love, This is what I sell.
Faith, Hope, Love, This is what I sell.
Faith, Hope, Love, This is what I sell.

2. The challenge of living, well, it's a big one.
To be alive and pleased with what you are.
They'll be both ups and downs;
The smiles and the frowns.
The dreams I'll really reach that special star.
I'll really reach that special star.
I'm gonna reach that special star!
Yes, I AM!

**CHORUS**

3. **Faith,** to keep believing without seeing.
**Hope** to carry on when life seems dark.
And **LOVE** that hangs around,
though problems do abound.
I'll keep these things and make my mark.
I'll keep these things and make my mark.
I'm gonna leave my special mark.
Yes, I AM!


My CD entitled, *Faith, Hope, and Love* is available for purchase through Amazon.com. These ten song were written shortly after my chemotherapy had ended. I think you will enjoy this music. Also, please visit my Website and Blog at www.drkayjg.com

# Epilogue - After 1979

*I'm alive and feeling free and I'm happy to be me.*
(From Faith, Hope, and Love by
Kay Johnson-Gentile)

I continued to change – and change a lot. Though I knew personal growth was helpful to me, it was not always helpful to my marriage. Sadly, as I dealt with breast cancer, I began growing in a much different direction than my husband.

After facing the possibility of my own death and working at Roswell Park with children and families dealing with the trauma of cancer, I was simply not the same young woman Bill had married. I was growing away from what my husband wanted and needed and vice versa.

It is not surprising that during cancer experiences families change. Divorce is common when dealing with cancer scenarios, especially when the woman is the cancer patient. Bill and I found ourselves more and more in conflict. The conflict was brought on by the intenseness of dealing with a disease like cancer and dissension from my becoming a different person – **a stronger, more, independent woman who was consumed with looking for spiritual meaning and purpose in life.**

When I finally knew that divorce was inevitable, I felt awful. I did not dislike Bill; I just realized I could no longer be his wife. How very sad to realize this, since who in their right mind would want to go through a divorce right after a bout with cancer? Who would want to know that their actions would be hurtful to others, especially their beautiful children and family? But, by the end of 1979 Bill and I were divorced.

We would always remain friends, though. Making a good life for our boys was more important than any differences we had. I will be forever grateful to Bill Johnson for being such a good friend and father. Tim and Chris adored him.

It has now been forty-one years since that fateful year of 1975. I AM still ALIVE! Yes, I am actually around and telling my story. I am one of the lucky ones and am so grateful for that.

It is ironic, however, that the very chemotherapy that helped save my life -- allowing me to grow as a woman -- would have horrible long-term side effects. These side effects would leave me disabled and would be responsible for my retiring from my job as a college professor at age fifty-eight.

What none of us knew back then was that the powerful chemo being administered to me in all probability began a destructive process of bone deterioration which would end up with me developing severe osteoporosis. My spinal column began a process of slow collapse which continues to this day. Over time, this resulted in my developing severe degenerative scoliosis and neuropathy, as well as dealing daily with severe chronic pain issues that required me to take powerful pain medications.

In spite of my health issues, I have had an amazing and full life. I had lots of *sunshine* moments all of which helped me actualize myself as a woman and mother. Getting my Ph.D. from The University at Buffalo; becoming a college Professor of Education; having amazing sabbatical leaves in China, Ireland, and Australia; receiving the State University of New York's (SUNY) Chancellor's Award for Excellence in Teaching in 2003; composing over thirty original songs;

having numerous written publications; teaching a workshop on Conflict Resolution at the Chautauqua Institute in Western New York; and finally, at age 63 becoming a Spiritual Director and teacher at the St. Joseph Center for Spirituality in Clarence, New York. All these things made the fabric of my life. For all this I am grateful.

Some of you may be wondering what happened to my father, Norris Burgher, and my beautiful mother, Nadine. Well, Dad died of pancreatic cancer in 1978, just three short years after my own cancer battle. Mom lived nearly twenty-five more years, passing away of a heart attack in 2004. But to me, they will *always be with me in spirit*, as well as through the many lessons they taught.

My father would frequently share with us kids inspiring adages or wise sayings. He did this especially during the tough, challenging times our family experienced. One of his favorites – and one he truly believed and practiced is -- *"It life gives you a lemon, make lemonade."*

Throughout his life, he was an example to all of us on how to make lemonade, but especially during his last two years as he gallantly dealt with pancreatic cancer. On the last day of his life, Dad was in the hospital and aware he was dying. With help he got up, showered, shaved and joked with the nurses. When he was, as he would say -- *presentable* – he lay back down in bed and passed out of this world and into the next. Dad was one of the most *courageous* men I ever knew. And following his example of *courage* is what I am trying my best to do now.

To catch you up with my children, Christopher, became a lawyer and is living with his wonderful family in Lockport, New York. Five years ago my husband and I moved to Lockport to be close to them.

The year 2012 was the **saddest year of my life.** My spirited son, Timothy, passed away. I still cannot talk about it. It is just too painful.

Three years ago in 2013, as my spinal degeneration worsened and I was needing to spend more and more time in bed, my husband and I purchased an adjustable bed. We then bought the perfect *over the bed table*, designed by a disabled person. This table became my new desk, so I could spend quality time in bed – doing what I love best now– writing.

*Using my Over Bed Table to Write*

I so enjoy writing my short stories of the heart -- *memoir* -- intended to *encourage and inspire* readers. Drawn from nearly seventy-four years of living, they provide touching accounts of my life and my amazing early years growing up in Moberly, Missouri. Writing has *given life back to me*.

As I type away, creating one of my stories, in the background are the most beautiful sounds -- musical sounds that continue to uplift and inspire me. And, yes, after all these years I am still listening to my old friend, John Denver.

People who know my story often ask me how the death of John Denver affected me. Like everyone else I was completely shocked. He was so young – only fifty-three years old. But to me, John never died. I say this because I can still play his music. It continues to comfort and inspire me. *Whenever* I hear someone mention the name, John Denver, I *always* break into a big smile. I loved this man.

My love for classical music has also continued. In fact, upon entering our little villa in Lockport, New York, you might hear the heavenly sounds of a Beethoven symphony, a Bach prelude, a Mozart piano concerto, a Rachmaninoff Variation, or a Wagner opera.

You might even hear an Alan Jackson song, Don Williams's mellow voice, or multi-talented Allison Kraus singing. I was raised country, and I still love country music. Yes, indeed, music will *always* be an important part of my life.

At least for now, I hear someone whispering in my ear, "Katie, this is **now** the time for you to write all your personal 'stories of the heart'--all the stories you and your loved ones created over a lifetime. Your **Walk of Faith, Hope, and Love** is not yet finished. You still need to complete this final task."

Be blessed, dear readers.

Kay

A book you will never forget! Just thinking of Kay's life and how she has served others regardless of her own pain brings tears of reverence for such an indomitable, highly talented woman! Read MY WALK OF FAITH, HOPE, & LOVE and allow it to inspire you to achieve greater heights! Your life will never be the same because Kay demonstrates the effectiveness of living in attunement with "I can do all things through Christ who strengthens me." Philippians 4-13
**Nancy B. Detweiler, Author**

Printed in the United States
By Bookmasters